LET'S VISIT BARBADOS

Let's visit
BARBADOS

R and V POTTER

ACKNOWLEDGEMENTS

The Authors and Publishers are grateful to the Barbados Board of Tourism for permission to reproduce copyright material in this book.

The Authors thank Graham and Elizabeth Dann for their continuing advice, encouragement and hospitality.

First published 1988

Published by
MACMILLAN PUBLISHERS LTD
Houndmills, Basingstoke, Hampshire RG21 2XS
and London
Companies and representatives
throughout the world

Designed and produced by Burke Publishing Company Limited
Pegasus House, 116-120 Golden Lane
London EC1Y 0TL, England.

Printed in Hong Kong

British Library Cataloguing in Publication Data
Potter, Robert B.
    Let's visit Barbados.
    1.   Barbados—Social life
    I.   Title   II.   Potter, V.
    972.98'1
    ISBN 0-333-46989-5

Contents

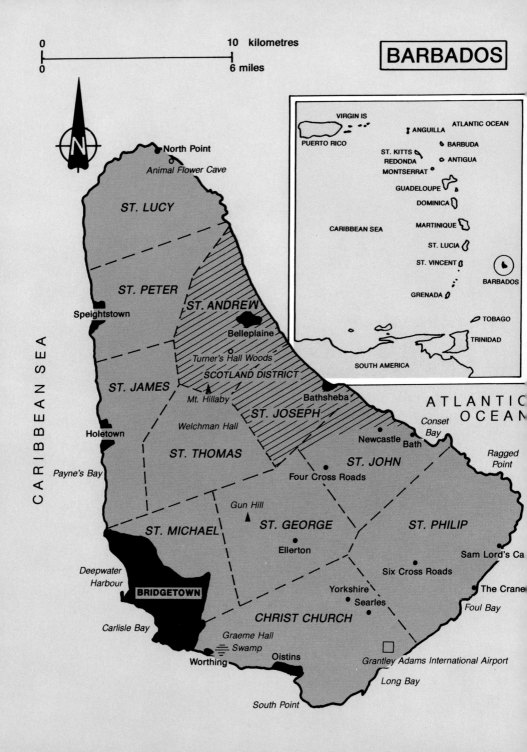

BARBADOS

0 ──────── 10 kilometres
0 ──────── 6 miles

N

North Point
Animal Flower Cave

ST. LUCY

ST. PETER

Speightstown

ST. ANDREW

Belleplaine

Turner's Hall Woods

SCOTLAND DISTRICT

ST. JAMES

Mt. Hillaby

Bathsheba

ST. JOSEPH

Holetown

Welchman Hall

Conset Bay

Newcastle   Bath

Payne's Bay

ST. THOMAS

Ragged Point

Four Cross Roads

ST. JOHN

Gun Hill

ST. GEORGE

ST. PHILIP

CARIBBEAN SEA

ST. MICHAEL

Ellerton

Sam Lord's Ca

Six Cross Roads

Deepwater Harbour

Yorkshire   The Crane

BRIDGETOWN

Searles

Foul Bay

Carlisle Bay

CHRIST CHURCH

Graeme Hall
Swamp

Oistins

Worthing

Grantley Adams International Airport

Long Bay

South Point

ATLANTIC OCEAN

VIRGIN IS

ANGUILLA   ATLANTIC OCEAN

PUERTO RICO

BARBUDA

ST. KITTS   ANTIGUA
REDONDA
MONTSERRAT

GUADELOUPE

DOMINICA

CARIBBEAN SEA

MARTINIQUE

ST. LUCIA

ST. VINCENT

BARBADOS

GRENADA

TOBAGO

TRINIDAD

SOUTH AMERICA

"Little England"?

The name Barbados comes from the Portuguese *Los Barbados,* which means "the bearded ones". It has been suggested that this name was given to the island by Portuguese sailors who were the first Europeans to sight it from out at sea. From their vantage point, they could see growing on the island the large tropical trees known as bearded figs. These trees look as though they have beards because of the lianas (or vines) which hang down from their branches in long trailing strands.

Barbados is one of a chain of islands stretching from Miami at the southern tip of the United States to the northern coast of South America close to Venezuela. Together, this area is referred to as the Caribbean or the West Indies.

This group of islands was first discovered by the European explorer Christopher Columbus in 1492. He thought that the world was round and not flat as many people believed at the time. In looking for a westward passage from Europe to India, his ship landed in the Caribbean at Watling Island in the

The east coast of Barbados — the first sight of the Caribbean for tourists and travellers arriving from Europe or Africa

Bahamas. Thinking that they had indeed reached India, the crew called the islands the "Indies". When their mistake was realized, the description "West Indies" seemed a suitable one. Nowadays, the term "Caribbean" is more often used to describe the region. This comes from the name of the Carib Indians of South America who were one of the first groups to live in the area.

The islands located in the eastern part of the Caribbean region are described as the Lesser Antilles. The Lesser Antilles are themselves divided into an inner and an outer group of islands. The inner islands make a broad curve from Grenada, through to St Vincent, St Lucia, Martinique, Dominica, Guadeloupe and north to Antigua. The outer chain is made up by Trinidad and

8

Tobago in the south, and Barbados in the north. Barbados' nearest neighbours, St Vincent and St Lucia, are located about 160 kilometres (100 miles) to the west.

The map of the Caribbean region shows, therefore, that Barbados is the most easterly of all the West Indian islands. This has been of considerable importance to its development through the ages. Its exact position is at latitude 13° 4' north and longitude 59° 37' west.

The shape of the island can be likened to that of a butterfly at rest, or even to that of a pear. It is quite small and measures approximately 34 kilometres (21 miles) from north to south, and 23 kilometres (14 miles) from east to west at its widest point. Overall, Barbados covers an area of 430 square kilometres (166 square miles).

Although located in the tropics, and separated from Europe by approximately 6,000 kilometres (4,000 miles), Barbados has come to be known as "Little England in the tropics". From 1627, for a period of almost 350 years, Barbados was an English colony. In this respect it differed from many of the other Caribbean islands which came under the rule of a number of different countries. It is because of this and the nature of the landscape, that Barbados is so often likened to England, the "Mother Country", or former colonial power.

Barbados is certainly a lot flatter than most other Caribbean islands. Much of the country is made up of gently rolling hills which have been divided into fields and used for agriculture—especially for growing sugar-cane—for centuries. As a result, viewed from the air, the patchwork of fields, crops and villages set on undulating land makes Barbados look to some people like southern England, rather than a tropical island.

But the comparison with England goes much further, and is extended to the people, the way they act and their values. It is also applied to other aspects of Barbados such as its culture, education system, form of government and legal system. Thus, the country is sometimes referred to as "Bimshire", implying that it is almost an English county or "shire".

The language of Barbados is English—but it is English spoken with a strong accent. However, a large number of local phrases and expressions are used in everyday conversation. Many English-speaking visitors find the resulting Bajan dialect very difficult to understand. (The word *Bajan* is used to describe all things Barbadian.)

It is also true that many places in the eleven parishes of Barbados have English names. They include the towns and villages of Worthing, Hastings, Yorkshire, Newmarket, Vauxhall, Henley, Newcastle, Cambridge, Oxford, Durham and Cheltenham, and there are many many more.

Statues recording past events also remind the visitor of the strength of this past association with England. These include the monument to Admiral Nelson which dominates Trafalgar Square in the capital city of Bridgetown. This was erected in 1813, twenty-seven years before the one in London, England. Another example is the lion carved out of limestone rock at Gun Hill by English troops stationed on the island in 1868.

The monument to Admiral Nelson in Bridgetown's Trafalgar Square

The comparison with England also reflects the long history of stable, peaceful and democratic government that Barbados has enjoyed. The country has the third oldest parliament in the Commonwealth. It dates from 1639. Only the British parliament in Westminster and the House of Assembly in Bermuda were established before it.

In 1966, Barbados became an independent nation within the British Commonwealth. But its constitution and government remain firmly based on the British system. The Head of State is the Queen (or King) of England, who is represented on the island by a Governor-General.

In fact, Barbados is one of the few Commonwealth nations

11

The lion carved out of limestone rock at Gun Hill

that has retained the "Westminster system" of government. Its parliament consists of two houses. First there is the Senate with twenty-one members. These are mainly approved by the Governor-General on the advice of the Prime Minister and the leader of the opposition. Secondly, the House of Assembly has twenty-seven members who are elected for a five-year term. There are two main political parties, the Barbados Labour Party and the Democratic Labour Party.

However, the similarities between Barbados and Britain should not be stressed too much, as evidenced by the national

12

flag adopted when the country gained independence. This consists of three vertical panels in blue, gold and blue. The top of a broken trident (three-pronged fork) is shown in black on the central gold panel. The trident represents the one usually held by Britannia as a symbol of the power of Britain overseas. Thus, the panel is a sign of the breaking of Barbados' past colonial ties with Britain.

Another obvious difference is the weather. Although Barbados may look a little less exotic than some other Caribbean islands, it is located in the region of the world called the tropics. This is the area of the earth around the equator where temperatures are generally hot throughout the year. More precisely, the zone extends between the Tropic of Cancer at 23½°North and the Tropic of Capricorn at 23½°South. Barbados has relatively high temperatures throughout the year, but they are never extreme. Temperatures average around 29 degrees Celsius (84 degrees Fahrenheit) during the day, and seldom if ever fall below 23 degrees Celsius (74 degrees Fahrenheit), even at night-time. What are known as the "trade winds" blow fairly constantly from the north-east. These prevent the island from getting too hot. The hottest period is during the wet or rainy season which lasts from around June to December. It is noticeably cooler and less humid from January to May—the dry season.

Only hurricanes (intense storms) pose a real climatic threat. These can develop over the Atlantic Ocean from July through to September. Although most hurricanes tend to travel through the Caribbean region somewhat to the north of Barbados, this is not always the case. Over the years, a number of hurricanes have damaged the island. More recently, in 1955, Barbados was hit by Hurricane Janet. In 1980, Hurricane Allen passed very close to the island.

Although it is a small country with limited resources, Barbados has for many years supported a relatively large population. In 1986, the total resident population was 253,055. On average, there are as many as 579 Barbadians living on every square kilometre (1,500 per square mile) of the island.

Over ninety per cent of the population are black. These people are the direct descendants of West Africans who, from the seventeenth century onward, were forced to work in Barbados as slaves. Barbados, therefore, has a strong African heritage. The value of this has only come to be appreciated since the country gained independence.

Some 3.3 per cent of the population are classified as white. Many people in this group are from families that originally owned and controlled large farms and businesses in Barbados. Over the last thirty years, members of the black majority have become the political leaders of the country. On the other hand, a small group of white people still own much of the land, business and wealth. But by no means all of the white population are rich. There is a group of poor whites, known locally as "Redlegs". They are the descendants of Scottish, Irish and Welsh people who came to work in the island early in its history. They got their name because the strong tropical sun tended to burn their legs

The aftermath of Hurricane Allen—rough water on the normally calm Caribbean Sea, off the west coast of Barbados

when they worked out in the open. The rest of the population is made up of small groups of mixed and East Indian races.

But whatever the colour of their skin, and no matter from which parish of the island they happen to come, Barbadians seem to share a number of characteristics. Perhaps first among these is pride. This may have something to do with Barbados' position—slightly to the east and away from the main chain of islands. Barbados is frequently described as either "the outsider of the Caribbean", or "a singular island".

Barbadians also pride themselves on their industry and

discipline. From very early on, right up to the present, there were few ways of earning a living in Barbados, other than the back-breaking work involved in growing sugar-cane. Barbadians are also reckoned to be sober, serious-minded, literate, well-educated and basically traditional in their views, being resistant to change for its own sake. They are frequently very self-assured—a feature that sometimes leads West Indians from other islands to claim that they are smug!

But there are many things about which Barbadians have every right to be proud. Certainly, their excellence at the game of cricket is well-known wherever in the world the game is played. Cricket is not just a sport in Barbados, it is a national obsession. It is played here, there and everywhere. Often homemade bats and stumps are used, especially in games played on waste land or on the beach. Barbados is also famous for its excellent rum, and as an attractive island for tourists. The sunny and warm climate, bright blue seas and golden beaches all combine to make Barbados a very popular place for holidaymakers.

Until the 1960s, the economy was largely based on the export of sugar. But, in the last twenty years, Barbados has made great economic progress. Today, tourism and light manufacturing industries are the chief money-earners. Barbados currently has one of the highest incomes per head of the population in the entire Caribbean.

On the other hand, life can still be harsh and very demanding for those who are less prosperous. Although Barbados is changing, it is still one of the poorer countries of the world.

Together, these countries are often described as the "Third World" or the "Developing Countries". Some of the problems which Barbados faces today have their origins in the things that happened or did not happen in the past. Thus, although it is interesting to talk of Barbados as "Little England", this description is too simple. Today, Barbados is a complex and rapidly-changing country. Quite simply, the details of its past history make it unique.

The Landscape

The landscape of Barbados today is the outcome of a complex series of events which occurred way back in time. Most Caribbean islands were formed by the activities of volcanoes. But Barbados is made up of rocks formed from sediments deposited at the bottom of seas which covered the area millions of years ago.

Rocks formed in this way are called sedimentary. One such rock, coral limestone, today forms eighty-five per cent of the land surface of Barbados. This was created from the crushed and compacted skeletons of millions of creatures, known as coral polyps, which live and grow in shallow warm seas. Other types of sedimentary rocks such as clays, sandstone and shales make up the remaining fifteen per cent of the surface of Barbados.

Barbados might be described as a cake formed of three layers of sedimentary rocks. Coral limestone, which formed more recently than the other rocks of Barbados, is found on top of a layer of clay-like rocks. In turn, these cover a series of older clays,

18

sandstones and shales. Put in the simplest terms, these three layers were deposited one on top of the other under a former sea.

After all this had happened, the rocks were raised up by a series of earth movements to form the island that we today call Barbados. The land was slowly lifted up in the shape of a dome. It reached a maximum height of around 300 metres (1,000 feet) in the centre of the island. A map of Barbados shows the highest point on the island is Mount Hillaby, which stands at 340 metres (1,115 feet). Mount Hillaby is at the top of the coral limestone rocks. From here, the land slopes down to the sea in all directions.

Another major feature of the land is a series of clear steps cut in the landscape, with relatively level land between them. These step-like features are called terraces, and they are most noticeable on the west side of the island where they run from north to south. They are also found in the area known as the Christ Church dome, where they run in an east to west direction. In fact, these terraces are old cliffs which were cut by the sea when the land was lower. They are evidence of the way in which the land has gradually been raised.

Compared with other Caribbean islands, the areas of Barbados which are covered by limestone are relatively flat. The limestone area is very large and in places reaches a maximum thickness of some 100 metres (300 feet).

The scenery found in such areas is very interesting, mainly because water runs down through it, rather than flowing across its surface. As a result, no permanent rivers are to be found in

Sugar-cane growing in a doline—a circular depression in the surface of the limestone which forms the top layer of rock

these areas. The mild acids which rainwater contains tend to dissolve limestone. Because of this, there are cracks through which water runs into the ground. These are called "sink holes". In other places, features called "dolines" occur. They are circular depressions in the surface of the limestone.

There are also some large underground caves formed where the coral limestone has been dissolved away. One such series of caves has been opened up and developed as a tourist attraction. This is Harrison's Cave located close to the centre of the island in the parish of St Thomas. Visitors are taken around the caves in an electric tram. One cave is 90 metres (295 feet) in length.

Although there are no rivers in these limestone areas, there are many steep-sided valleys which appear to have been cut by

20

rivers in the past. Water must have flowed along these so-called "dry valleys" at some time in the past, but it is not fully understood when and how this happened.

The limestone covering has been stripped away from the north-eastern part of the island. Where this rock ends there is what is known as the Great Limestone Cliff. The southern part, called Hackleton's Cliff, is very steep. In places it towers 300 metres (1,000 feet) above the area of the east coast where the older sandstones and clays are exposed. The landscape in this 57 square-kilometre (23 square-mile) area is very different from

A view of a dry valley

Gully formation and soil erosion in the Scotland District

that found in other parts of the island. It is so rugged and hilly that it is called the Scotland District, on account of its similarity to the highland areas of Scotland. Deep ravines have been carved in the clay areas, whilst the sandstones are a little more resistant and remain as knife-edged ridges. Severe soil erosion has occurred in many places such as, for example, the Joe's River basin.

There seems little doubt that human activities since the time of European colonization have made these problems much worse. When the English came to the island in 1625, it was covered with tropical forests. Only one small area of this forest remains today. This is at Turner's Hall Woods, in the parish of St Andrew.

The natural forest areas of Barbados were quickly cleared to allow crops to be grown. This left the ground more open to erosion than before, especially as a result of heavy rain. By the end of the seventeenth century, the problem had become so serious that it was no longer possible to grow sugar-cane in the Scotland District. Increasingly, the land was used to graze goats and sheep. Where areas were stripped of vegetation by these animals, the problem of erosion was made much worse. Great efforts are at present being made to reduce the effects of soil erosion and of landslides in this, the most rugged and hilly, area of the country.

The History of Barbados

Perhaps the most important fact concerning the past of Barbados is that its history is a relatively short one. Human beings have been known to live on the island only for the last 1,500 years.

The first people to live permanently in Barbados were Indians who originally came from South America. These peoples are referred to as Amerindians. The first such group to come to the island—the Barrancoid Indians—are believed to have reached it in around AD 400. They travelled to Barbados as a part of a slow process of movement from their homeland around the River Orinoco. From here they migrated northwards to what is present-day Venezuela, and then to Trinidad and the rest of the Caribbean. Remains of the highly decorated pottery that these people made have been found quite recently at South Point in Barbados.

The Barrancoid Indians seem to have lived in Barbados until around AD 600. There was then a gap of two hundred years

A beach which looks today much as it may have looked to the first inhabitants of Barbados, the Barrancoid Indians

before another group—this time Arawak Indians—came to the island. The Arawaks lived by fishing and growing crops such as cassava, maize, peanuts, squash and various fruits. (The name Arawak means "cassava-eater".) They made full use of the plentiful clays of the island to make pottery. Apparently, these peaceful Indians inhabited the island for four to five hundred years. But by AD 1200, they seem to have been conquered by the fierce and warlike people who gave their name to the region— the Carib Indians. These people are thought to have been cannibals, sometimes eating the enemies they captured.

The explorer Christopher Columbus did not find Barbados on any of the four voyages he made to the New World from 1492 onward. But later Portuguese and Spanish seamen came upon it. When Spaniards visited the island early in the 1500s, Caribs

25

were still living there. But by the time a Portuguese ship landed in 1536, none were to be found. It is now thought that the Spaniards transported them to work as slaves on the larger island of Hispaniola (now Haiti and the Dominican Republic). Also, on the arrival of the Europeans, the Caribs were suddenly exposed to killer diseases such as smallpox and tuberculosis, against which they had no defence.

Neither the Spaniards nor the Portuguese settled permanently on the island. Thus, when in 1625, an English ship came to Barbados by mistake, the members of the crew found it

The Holetown monument, commemorating the tercentenary of the landing of the crew of the British vessel *Olive Blossom*

uninhabited, apart from wild hogs that had been left as a source of food by the Portuguese in 1536. The vessel, the *Olive Blossom*, was captained by John Powell and when they landed on the west coast of the island, near to what is today Holetown, they claimed the island in the name of James I, King of England.

On returning home they told their employer, Sir William Courteen, about the island. He was impressed and decided to send a group of eighty people to settle there and grow crops. They arrived on 17 February, 1627, landing at the same place as the earlier group two years before.

For almost the next 350 years, Barbados was an English colony, with its development tied closely to England. The first settlement was named Jamestown, and the group set about clearing the land and planting crops. The settlers had with them ten black slaves who had been captured from trading-ships during the crossing from England. Tobacco, cotton, ginger and indigo were grown to sell for export, the profits going to Sir William Courteen.

Back in England, the Earl of Carlisle heard of the money being made. He set about convincing the new King Charles I to grant him the rights to Barbados and other Caribbean islands. In 1628, a year after the first settlement, Carlisle sent his own group of around sixty colonists to Barbados. They settled at what is now Bridgetown, landing near to present-day Carlisle Bay.

From these early days onward, economic profits dominated the history of Barbados. Due to competition from the United States of America, especially the state of Virginia, tobacco was

27

not as successful as had at first been hoped. Only twelve years after the first settlement, Pieter Blower, a Dutchman who had learned how to grow sugar-cane in Brazil, brought news of the crop to Barbados. A very swift change occurred. By 1642, Barbados had become the first British colony to produce sugar on a large scale.

The years from 1643 to 1700, are often referred to as the "sugar boom". This was a period when large profits were made. Sugar brought about two major changes which were to affect the whole future of the country. The first was the development of large farms—called plantations—to grow cane and produce sugar.

The second change—the introduction of black slaves—was just as important. As well as money, growing cane requires a great deal of work and effort. Holes have to be dug and pieces of cane planted in them. The fields have to be weeded and fertilized regularly. The cane has to be cut down and transported to mills where the sugar is extracted.

At first, indentured (contracted) labourers did most of the work. They were people who agreed to work for a plantation for five or seven years. In return, the cost of their journey to Barbados was paid. And, at the end of this period, some were given a plot of land, or the money with which to buy one.

A major change occurred when black slaves were imported to do this back-breaking work. Buying a slave who would have to work for life was cheaper than paying for an indentured labourer who would work for only a few years. So started a
28

cruel and harsh system of slavery which was to last for 150 years.

Men, women and young adults from West Africa were captured and taken to the Caribbean against their will. Chained by both hand and foot they were packed into the holds of ships in the most cramped, unhealthy conditions and shipped across from West Africa to the New World. Many died during the long and cruel voyage. On arrival, the survivors were sold as slaves to the highest bidder.

The conditions endured by the slaves were generally very harsh indeed. For example, killing a slave was considered to be only a minor offence carrying the punishment of a mere £15 fine. The slaves came from different areas of West Africa, and had different cultures and languages. This pleased the white planters, as it meant that the slaves were less able to talk to each other and plot a rebellion.

Barbados had changed into a "plantation society" where a small group of white planters controlled a black majority who were not free. The change was swift. In the 1630s, the black population had been only eight hundred. By 1643, the figure had reached six thousand, and by 1684 it was sixty thousand. By this time, the black slaves outnumbered their white masters by as many as three to one. Hence, any attempted uprising by slaves, and there were several in the years between 1683 and 1702, was dealt with in a very harsh manner. By the late 1600s, all free men were required to serve in a trained militia—a civilian force which became the chief weapon against slave rebellion.

Due to campaigns in England, led by social reformers such as

A young Barbadian. This man's ancestors were brought to the country against their will, from West Africa, as slaves

William Wilberforce, in 1807 the British parliament made the slave trade illegal. But it was not until 1834 that slavery itself was abolished. Even then, a four-year period of apprenticeship was introduced, so that only in 1838 could the seventy thousand labourers celebrate the gaining of their legal freedom.

When this "emancipation" happened, the planters were worried that their workers would be free to leave them, and that they might perhaps set up their own small farms. But, in reality, there was little chance of this. By this time virtually all the fertile lands in Barbados were already owned by the large plantations, so there was really no place where the freed slaves could set up their own smallholdings.

30

Further, a law was passed in 1840 which set out the conditions under which freed slaves were to be provided with rented houses on their master's land in return for the work they did on the plantations. But, if such workers were dismissed from their jobs, they could be turned off the land on which they lived. The landlord only had to give workers four weeks' notice to leave.

In these and many other ways, sugar-plantations and planters continued to dominate life in Barbados long after the emancipation of the slaves. The wages paid to workers remained very low indeed. Eventually, what the planters had always

A statue erected by the government and people of Barbados to commemorate the 150th anniversary of the abolition of slavery and the emancipation of Barbadians

worried about started to happen. During the period from 1850 to 1914, over twenty thousand Barbadians emigrated to Panama to work on the canal that was being constructed there. Others went to jobs in places such as Brazil, British Guiana (now Guyana), Trinidad, Costa Rica and Curaçao.

As Barbados entered the twentieth century, the conditions faced by workers at home showed little if any real signs of improvement. Wages remained very low and health, education and social services were generally very poor indeed. When a great economic depression affected the world in the 1930s, Barbados was badly hit. Eventually, in 1937, unhappy workers rioted in the streets of Barbados in order to protest about the conditions under which they were living. The disturbances lasted for three days and, during this time, fourteen people were killed and forty-seven injured.

But this period of hardship was followed by an era of social reform and change. In particular, the Barbados Labour Party was formed in 1938. In 1941, the Barbados Workers' Union was established. The aim of both these organizations was to improve the lives of poor workers. One man in particular—Grantley H. Adams, the leader of the Barbados Labour Party—was associated with this fight for greater equality. His son, Tom Adams, became the prime minister of Barbados in 1976, and held this post until his death in 1985.

During the years between 1958 and 1962, Barbados joined with a number of other Caribbean countries to form a federation. This was an idea which had been suggested many

A man taking water from a standpipe. While public services have improved in recent years, life is still not easy for working people in Barbados with little money to spare

years before (in 1876) as a way of tackling the economic problems faced by Caribbean countries. Unfortunately, for a number of reasons, this association did not work.

In 1961, the Democratic Labour Party came to power with Errol Barrow as its leader. In 1966, under his leadership, Barbados made its historic break with England, gaining its independence after three hundred years as a colony. At about the same time, tourism and manufacturing industry were both becoming very important economic activities in a nation where sugar had been undisputed king for three centuries.

Towns, Villages and Transport

The history of Barbados shows how the first two groups of settlers both landed on the western side of the island and built villages there. They selected this side of the island because it faces the Caribbean Sea. The trade winds blow across Barbados almost constantly from the east or north-east. Thus, the Caribbean Sea is generally very calm and smooth. In contrast, the eastern side of the island faces the full force of the Atlantic Ocean and is often very rough and stormy. Also, waves and winds have cut steep cliffs along many sections of this exposed sea coast.

This difference between the two sides of the island gives rise to a very important contrast. The exposed eastern part of Barbados is described as the "windward" side of the island. On the other hand, the sheltered and calm western parts are known as the "leeward". The physical structure of the island also means that there is more relatively flat land on the leeward side of the island, whilst the windward area is generally hillier.

The places which were developed by the early settlers in the 1600s have all continued to grow and are still the four main towns of the island. The first settlement, Jamestown, is now known as Holetown. Later, settlements were built at Bridge-town, Oistins and Speightstown.

At first, the place where the second group of settlers lived — what is now Bridgetown — was not regarded as a very good position. This was mainly because the land around it was low-lying and because the presence of large swampy areas close by presented a number of health problems, including that of malaria.

But the map of Barbados shows very clearly the many advantages of the site of Bridgetown. Early on, the most important was undoubtedly the wide and sheltered bay which occurs at this point on the coastline. This was given the name

A view of Bridgetown across the bay

Carlisle Bay by the early settlers, and it was clearly the best place at which to anchor ships and off-load their cargoes.

Just to the north of this wide bay, a narrow arm of the sea creates a natural harbour. This inlet is also known as the Constitution River, even though inland it is little more than a dry river valley. The inner part of this natural basin is called the Careenage—the place where boats are painted, repaired and overhauled.

In fact, it is because the early Indian inhabitants are thought to have built a bridge across this inlet that the town was given its name. At first, it was known as "Indian Bridge", or "Indian Bridgetown". Later this became "The Bridge" or "Bridgetown". As sugar flourished and plantations developed, Bridgetown was also a good place to act as a collection point for the sugar produced in the fertile inland areas of the island. Over time, therefore, Bridgetown became the chief port and commercial hub of the island—a position it retains today.

The fact that Barbados is so far to the east of the other Caribbean islands meant that Bridgetown became the first port of call for ships making their way from Europe to the West Indies. It became the place where commodities were shipped into the country from overseas, and the main place where goods were stored. Banks and financial institutions of all sorts grew here, and shops were also built in the city.

In the north of the island, Speightstown gradually developed into the second largest port. At one time, it was given the nickname "Little Bristol". This was because it was from here that

A view over Oistins Town and bay

the sugar which was produced in the northern and eastern parts of the island was shipped to the English port of Bristol.

The site of the first settlement, Holetown, did not have the same natural advantages of both Bridgetown and Speightstown. The same was also true of Oistins Town located in the south-east, for the stretch of coast along which it is built is far less protected and calm. However, Oistins did develop as a centre for the fishing industry.

Over time, these four main towns have slowly grown together. Thus, today, they form an almost continuous built-up area which stretches all the way along the west and south coasts, from Speightstown in the north right down to Oistins.

Outside this long and narrow built-up coastal area, agriculture is the main activity. Even away from the main towns, villages are very strongly clustered into particular areas.

The clustering is a result of the beginnings of the villages in the days of plantation slavery. Many plantation tenantries, where the workers lived, were built either at the edges or the corners of estates. Others were built close together on poor marginal areas known as "rab" land. In yet other cases, such houses were constructed along the main roads which ran at the sides of the fields. This pattern still influences a great deal of the present-day landscape of Barbados. It is also reflected in the compact villages which have grown at the junctions of roads in the agricultural areas. Good examples are provided by the present-day settlements of Four Cross Roads, Four Roads and Six Cross Roads. In many villages, even those in strongly agricultural areas, houses are built very close together. In some places they almost touch each other.

It was only the houses of the plantation-owners and managers that were built in more scattered and isolated places. Many of these plantation houses are large and grand dwellings which have survived to the present day. Some of them still perform the function for which they were originally built. But others have now been opened to the public. Plantation houses such as the earliest great house, Nicholas Abbey, built in around 1650, give an impression of the luxury in which the planters lived during the early days of the island's settlement by the British. Another famous plantation house, Villa Nova built in 1834 in the parish

Nicholas Abbey, a plantation house built in the middle of the seventeenth century — the earliest of the great houses

of St John, and once owned by Sir Anthony Eden, a former British prime minister, is also open for the public to visit.

Today, Bridgetown is the administrative and political capital of Barbados. It is regarded as a city, since St Michael's Cathedral, is located near the centre of Bridgetown. The Cathedral was originally built in 1665, and was reconstructed in 1831. In total, some 100,000 people live in the wider Bridgetown urban area. This means that the capital is home for around forty-two per cent of the nation's total population.

In Broad Street, the main commercial area, there are always crowds of shoppers visiting the large department stores and shopping malls such as Harrisons, DaCostas and Cave Shepherd. In fact, all the essential commercial services and

39

Broad Street, Bridgetown, with a view of Da Costa's

facilities are to be found in Bridgetown. These include lawyers, banks, merchants, warehouses, offices and places of entertainment such as the cinema. In addition, Bridgetown has two large markets—Cheapside and Fairchild Street—where fresh produce can be purchased. The House of Assembly is also located near the business centre of the city.

Bridgetown is the chief commercial centre and port of the Lesser Antilles. The inner part of the Careenage has been developed as a marina for pleasure craft. Overlooking it, old warehouses have recently been converted into a restaurant, bar and shopping complex called the Waterfront.

Although there are some areas of quite poor housing in Bridgetown, conditions in the urban zone are generally better than those found in the rural districts. Year by year, Bridgetown

40

is becoming more developed and modern. Recently, for example, new buildings have been constructed to house the Central Bank of Barbados and the General Post Office. A new fishing complex and market was also built during 1987-8.

The northern town of Speightstown and its surrounding area currently has a population of around ten thousand. A new central shopping area has been developed. In the middle-1980s, the Haywoods Beach tourist complex and Arawak cement works were opened. These are both located to the north of the town.

The new Central Bank building in Bridgetown

Halfway between Bridgetown and Speightstown is Holetown, very much the commercial centre for the west-coast tourist zone. Oistins, on the south coast of Barbados, acts as the shopping centre for the south-west and has a new fisheries market.

However, the day-to-day life of Barbados is very much concentrated on the Bridgetown area. Because Bridgetown is so much larger than any other single town, politicians and planners have generally argued that it is becoming too crowded and congested. It has been suggested that steps must now be taken to encourage new growth outside the city. But a great deal remains to be done if facilities for this are to be built in other parts of the island.

Congestion is one problem to be solved. It is caused by the

A residential area of Bridgetown

A view of the deepwater harbour from Cave Hill. Note the sugar-loaders and the cruise-ship

large numbers of people travelling into Bridgetown to work, shop, visit the cinema and make use of the city's other facilities. In fact, Barbados has one of the densest road networks in the world. There are 1,642 kilometres (1,020 miles) of roads. But the main roads—or highways as they are called locally—form a pattern rather like the spokes radiating from the centre of a wheel. Just as it is often said that in Italy "all roads lead to Rome", so in Barbados all roads lead to Bridgetown. Thus, although Barbados has an efficient and quite inexpensive system of blue-and-yellow buses and minibuses, it is often easier to get into Bridgetown than to travel even quite short distances across the island. In order to ease this problem, a highway was built around

43

A horsedrawn cart—still in use but a sign of the past

the edge of Bridgetown during the late 1980s. This runs from the international airport across to the north of Bridgetown and it links with the main highways which run out of the city.

Two very important developments since the 1960s have made Barbados a major centre for international transport in the eastern Caribbean. The first was the construction of a modern deepwater harbour. This opened in 1961 and is situated just to the north of the city. It was built on what was formerly Pelican Island, just off the coast, and on reclaimed land around it. The deepwater harbour has berths for eight ocean-going ships of 170-200 metres (500-600 feet) in length to anchor. It also has facilities for the bulk storage and loading of sugar. The other development was the construction of an ultra-modern terminal building at the Grantley Adams International Airport. The

44

airport now has all the facilities needed to handle the largest international aircraft.

Barbados has come a long way since the early days when the first settlers cleared the forests and set about making rough paths. In those days, they even used camels from West Africa and donkeys to carry them around the island. One of the things from the more recent past that is missed today is the Barbados Railway. It was opened in 1882 and, for fifty years or so, carried passengers between Bridgetown and the eastern side of the island. The path that the line took can still be followed along the east coast. But sadly, in 1937, due to economic pressures, the railway closed, thereby ending an era in the transport history of the island.

Everyday Life

The houses seen today in Barbados are very distinctive. When the last population census was carried out in 1980, there were just over 67,000 households within the country. At that time, as many as 38,000, or over half the population, lived in dwellings constructed entirely of wood. A further twelve per cent of the houses were made of wood together with concrete or brick. However, things are changing. Even as recently as 1970, over seventy-five per cent of all Barbadian houses were constructed solely of wood.

Still today, many basic houses are little more than small timber cabins. In fact, they may measure only six metres (twenty feet) by three metres (ten feet); and, in such a structure, a whole family of four, five, six or even more people may live.

These houses are built to a standard pattern which has been found in Barbados for many centuries. Their style results from the combination of types of house commonly found in southern England and West Africa during the period when Barbados was

46

A typical chattel house with a window on either side of the central door, and a rectangular plan

being settled in the seventeenth century. Firstly, the houses are rectangular in shape, so that they are roughly twice as long as they are wide. The house is normally built so that the long side faces directly on to the road or gap (as a small residential road is called). The main door is almost always located in the centre of the front of the house, and there are two windows, one on either side of it.

Many features help to keep houses cool by making the most of the local breezes. The use of wood itself helps to prevent the rooms from getting too hot. In traditional Barbadian houses, the windows are not made from glass. Instead, the window spaces are covered by wooden slats. These are called jalousies and they

47

allow air to pass through them even when they are shut. Canopies above the windows shade them from the overhead sun, and are referred to as box pelmets. The houses are painted in a bewildering variety of colours, but the pastel shades of pink, cream, green, blue and light brown are very common.

Perhaps one of the most interesting features of such houses is that they are often built upon a foundation of loose rocks which have been piled up on the plot of land, or house spot as it is called.

This type of house goes back to the plantation system. Workers on plantations were given house spots to rent during their period of employment. On these plantation tenantries, workers built their own houses. But if they were sacked, or moved to another job, they had to move their home. Hence, Barbadian homes were literally moveable possessions. As a result, even the present-day wooden dwellings are called "chattel houses"—homes that can be moved.

In fact, this way of moving house Barbadian-style, still occurs. At present, in any one year, around six hundred chattel houses are moved from one part of the island and rebuilt in another. The house is first taken down, side by side, and the panels are stacked to await removal by several trucks. Permission to do this is required from the Planning Office. In an effort to reduce disruption, such houses are normally moved to their new sites on a Sunday.

One of the great virtues of the traditional housing system of Barbados is that it is flexible. Not only can houses be moved, but

An extended and converted chattel house in St John

they can be extended and improved as families grow or fortunes change. Normally, this is done by joining on a second, third or even fourth wooden unit behind the original one. In recent years, there has been a tendency for people to add a toilet and bathroom at the back of the house, this being built of concrete or brick.

If well maintained, chattel houses are very sound and possess a charm and beauty all of their own. But in a hot and humid climate, unless the wood has been properly treated with preservatives in the first place and then painted regularly, rot, termites and other insects can soon cause them to crumble and decay.

As a result, many new houses are built in concrete or brick. In addition, some people convert their wooden houses by building around them with concrete blocks. Another development is that, since the 1950s, the government of Barbados has built approximately three thousand homes. These rented houses, which are looked after by the National Housing Corporation, are all wall structures, built of brick or concrete. By contrast, many of the more prosperous people in Barbados live in large bungalow-style houses built on the top of the ridges and terraces where the views are good.

Current housing policies aim to encourage people to improve and upgrade their homes. A special Act of Parliament passed in 1980 gives people living in chattel houses on plantation tenantries the right to buy the land on which their home is built. It is hoped that this will lead to the building of better and more permanent homes.

The influence of the plantation system can also be seen in other areas of everyday life. Many slave-masters prevented or discouraged slaves from marrying. Later on, economic hardship meant that men often went to live and work overseas, either permanently or seasonally.

The result is that the family system of Barbados is adapted to fathers being away from the home. Thus, although the family system is strong and very important, it is a flexible and open one. Almost sixty per cent of the population over fourteen years of age have never been married. In fact, seventy-eight per cent of children are born outside legal marriages, but little social importance is attached to illegitimacy, and parents may well marry long after they have reared children. As elsewhere in the Caribbean, when weddings do take place, they are normally grand and very costly affairs.

The major characteristic of Barbadian family-life is the mother-centred household. This pattern is well explained by the title of a book written about the Caribbean by Edith Clarke called *My Mother Who Fathered Me*. Mothers generally take the prime responsibility for raising their children. If mothers have to work, then children are usually looked after by grandmothers, or other female relatives. This system is made easier by the fact that different generations of the same family often live together in extended chattel houses.

An important trend affecting Barbados is a reduction in the

**A mother and her child
in rural St Peter**

number of children people have. Although in the past families tended to be very large, since the mid-1950s the government has encouraged people to limit their families. This has been very successful and, today, Barbados has a population growth-rate of only 0.2 per cent per year, which is low for a developing country.

Progress has also been made in other areas of life, especially health and social services. In the early years, Barbados was a far from healthy place and many people died as a result of dysentery, typhoid, smallpox, yellow fever and other diseases. Until recently, however, there was no health or social welfare programme and many poor people had to fend for themselves as best they could.

Today, however, treatment is free at the 600-bed Queen Elizabeth Hospital. This is located in the centre of Bridgetown and was opened in 1964. In the last few years, real efforts have been made to provide more health facilities outside the city and there are now ten government health centres, called polyclinics, where treatment is also free. In addition, there are well over one hundred doctors who can be consulted privately by those who can afford to pay their fees. There are also several private hospitals.

Life expectancy has increased greatly in Barbados since the Second World War (1939-1945). The average age to which people live is now around seventy years. In part, this is due to the better health-care facilities that are currently available. But improvement in the overall standard of living has also been important. Today, the main causes of death in Barbados are heart disease, various cancers, sugar diabetes and road accidents.

Another aspect of day-to-day Barbadian life where the blending of African, English and other influences can be seen is in the food people eat. Barbadian cooking is inventive and reflects not only the local produce available, but also the need to make ends meet. Because the country is an island, fish forms a very important part of the diet. What are known as flying fish are prepared seasoned with herbs, spices and lime juice. They are frequently served with a side dish called *cou-cou*—a pudding made from cornmeal and okra. Served together, flying fish and *cou-cou* are regarded as the national dish of Barbados. Other fish found in the waters around the island include red snapper, king fish, chub and dolphin. "Sea-eggs", the roe or eggs of the female sea urchin, are another local delicacy. Pork is also eaten a great deal, especially when pickled, as in the local dish called "pudding and souse".

A range of vegetables, either fresh or pickled, appears on most tables. A well-known main course consists of peas and rice mixed together. The breadfruit, a large starchy green-skinned fruit which grows on trees, is also very popular. Despite its name, the inside of the breadfruit tastes more like potato than bread. It can be fried, boiled, stewed or pickled. Other popular vegetables include sweet potato, yam, eddoes and cassava.

The various fruits grown on the island—limes, cherries, guavas, mangoes, gooseberries, passion fruit, pawpaws, soursops and coconut among them—are used to produce fruit drinks and punches. Another local drink, called Mauby, is made by boiling the bitter bark of a type of tree. The mixture is then sweetened and spiced. But it is rum, made as a by-product of sugar, which is the main drink at social gatherings. Barbadians talk of rum being "fired", not drunk. Rum is the base of a local liqueur, called falernum, which also includes lime juice, sugar, water and almond essence. When falernum is mixed with rum, the result is known as "corn and oil".

All over the island, small premises called rum shops are to be found. They sell rum, beer and other alcoholic drinks. In the evenings, they act as important meeting-places for men wishing to drink. There are approximately one thousand rum shops in Barbados. They are also important because many of them act as ordinary shops, stocking things like canned and packeted foods. In the rural areas, the rum shop may be the only grocery store.

A breadfruit tree and a coconut palm

A rum shop

Another important form of selling is performed by "hawkers", generally women, who sell fruit, vegetables, nuts and other items from small trays which they set up in the street. Very often these women live in rural areas and travel to places in town to sell their produce.

But, as elsewhere, large supermarkets are becoming an important part of daily life in Barbados. Supermarkets were first built in Barbados in the late 1960s, at a time when tourism was increasing. Today, virtually all the large stores of this kind are located on the outskirts of Bridgetown. They mainly attract people who are able to use a car to do their shopping.

In this, as in so many other respects, Barbados today and the lives of its residents are very much a combination of the old and the new, the traditional and the modern.

Sugar and Other Products

Barbados has been described as "a city where sugar-cane grows in the suburb". In fact, sugar-cane still dominates the landscape outside the towns, as it has done for over three centuries. Today, sugar-cane is grown on eighty-five per cent of the total crop land. In the past, Barbados lived mainly from sugar, and its by-products—molasses and rum. Even now, sugar is the main crop, although production has fallen from 180,000 tonnes in 1966, to around 100,000 tonnes at present.

Sugar-cane was originally introduced during the seventeenth century, and Barbados is well-suited to growing it. The land is relatively flat and the soil is well-drained. The warm temperatures, high rainfall and clear wet and dry seasons are ideal for the growth of cane.

Growing sugar-cane requires large areas of land. As a result, Barbados soon became divided into large holdings, or plantations. To produce sugar, many plantation-owners built sugar-mills on their own land. Large numbers of workers were needed to grow the cane and operate the sugar-mills and so the cruel system of slavery was introduced. Today, there are some reminders of these early days in the plantations which still exist and in the ruins of the sugar-mills.

There are still 130 large estates, where most of the sugar is produced. In addition, there are 15,000 small farms. Today, many food crops are grown and livestock is kept. Sugar-production, as well as farming in general, has become more mechanized, and only about nine per cent of the workforce are now employed in farming.

Sugar-cane is a tall grass which grows up to four metres (twelve feet) in height and has a stem about four centimetres (1.5 inches) thick. It is usually grown from cuttings which are planted out in November, at the end of the wet season. It takes up to seventeen months to reach maturity. The cane is ready for harvesting eighteen months after planting. The next crop grows from the stumps that are left after the harvest. These new shoots are called ratoons. Because different areas of sugar-cane are at different stages of growth, Barbados always seems to have a landscape of waving canes.

During the growing season, the canes are weeded and sprayed. Harvesting takes place at the beginning of the dry season in February, and lasts through to June. Until recently, most cane was cut by field-workers using long knives called machetes. Traditionally, to make cane-cutting easier, the cane was set on fire to burn away the dry leaves. However, this can have a damaging effect on the soil. Nowadays, it is quite common

Sugar-cane—introduced into Barbados in the seventeenth century and grown on plantations

to see large machines, known as cane-cutters, in the fields. These cut the canes at ground level. The field-workers then remove the tops of the canes and pile them up ready for collection. The canes are then taken to the factories by truck.

In the past, sugar-cane was ground in windmills. These were introduced into Barbados by the Dutch in the seventeenth century. At one time there were five hundred sugar windmills on the island. The best remaining example is the Morgan Lewis windmill in St Andrew.

Today, sugar is produced at six factories on the island. On

arrival at the factory the cane is cut into pieces and crushed to extract the juice. In the last part of the crushing process, water is sprayed on the canes to wash out any remaining juice. The juice is then clarified to remove impurities. The water is evaporated, leaving a thick brown syrup which is boiled in large pans. Crystals start to form in the syrup, or molasses as it is called. The mixture is transferred to huge spinners which separate the sugar crystals from the molasses. The sugar is then sent by truck to the sugar stores and loaders at the deepwater harbour at

The Morgan Lewis windmill in St Andrew

**Sugar-loading towers
in the Bridgetown
harbour**

Bridgetown. From here, much of the sugar is exported by ship to many other countries. The rest is sold locally.

Bagasse—the material left after the canes have been crushed—is used to feed animals and to make hardboard. The other by-product—molasses—is mainly used in the production of rum, but is also used to make black treacle and animal feed.

Rum is made by distilling the juice from molasses. It is believed that the name rum was invented in Barbados. At first it was called "rumbullion", due to the "rumbustious" and "rebellious" feelings it was said to have encouraged among those who drank

60

it. It was also known as "kill-devil" due to its strength. In fact, Barbados was the first country to export rum. Today, there are two rum factories on the island; and these produce the famous Mount Gay and Cockspur rums.

For many years Barbados produced few crops other than sugar, although some food crops have always been planted after the sugar harvest. Alternatively, such crops have been planted between the canes—a practice called inter-cropping. As a result of the large area of land devoted to sugar, Barbados has always imported many food crops and much of its meat. Over recent years, the government has been trying to reduce dependence on sugar by encouraging farmers to produce more food crops. At present, around twelve per cent of the land is used to grow other crops, and at least half of this is on small farms.

Small-holders now produce a wide range of vegetables, such as yams, sweet potatoes, aubergines, breadfruit, eddoes and hot peppers, some of which are exported. Other crops, such as peas, beans and maize, are also produced and the island is now self-sufficient in onions, tomatoes and carrots. Fruit production, including water-melons, bananas, coconuts, mangoes, avocados, and cherries, is also increasing. In addition, tropical flowers, such as the red ginger lily, are grown for export.

Cotton was grown briefly in Barbados when the island was first settled, but this soon ceased. In 1983, it was reintroduced as a commercial crop and sea-island cotton is now exported, especially to Japan.

There are also signs of increasing diversification in livestock production. In 1985, there were eighteen thousand cattle, fifty-four thousand sheep and thirty-two thousand goats on the island. Most small farmers keep a few animals, especially for milk. But there are now several large dairy herds producing milk for the local market. Pig- and poultry-rearing is also increasing. But, even today, Barbados imports as much as eighty per cent of all the meat consumed.

A number of industries have been developed to produce food for the local market. These agro-industries include the packaging of vegetables, and the production of hot pepper sauce, fruit juices, milk and dairy products.

Fish is another important source of food and there are about one thousand full-time fishermen in Barbados. Flying fish form a large part of the catch, although they are only found in the waters close to the island from December to June. Many other kinds of fish are caught, including dolphin, red snapper, barracuda, shark, king fish, tuna and bream. In 1985, there were about 650 powered fishing-boats, and the total catch was approximately 6,000 tonnes. Shrimps are also caught off the South American coast and are exported to the USA and Japan as well as to other Caribbean islands.

The production of food for local consumption is vital to a densely populated country like Barbados. Although sugar is decreasing in importance to the economy, it is certain to remain as the main crop. But the government regards sugar as only one part of a diversified system of agriculture, which includes local food-producing industries.

A small herd such as many Barbadian farmers keep

However, a number of problems have to be faced if agriculture is to be further diversified. One is the pressing need to encourage people to have a more positive view of agricultural work after its long historical association with slavery and low wages. Others include maintaining soil fertility and reducing erosion. Finally, if the local production of certain food and tree crops is to be increased, this will require irrigation—an expensive process in a country like Barbados.

Plants and Animals

Most plants and animals found in Barbados today have been introduced since the island was settled by the English in 1627. Much of the original plant and animal life was wiped out as the land was cleared for settlement and farming.

Colourful trees and shrubs cover much of the island. Of these, the bright scarlet or yellow flowers of the flamboyant tree are said to be the most beautiful in the tropics. Other flowering trees include the sweet-smelling frangipani, the scarlet cordia, and the yellow and pink cassias. Throughout Barbados, large shade trees such as the tamarind, the mahogany and the tall conifer-like casuarina have been planted.

Along the beaches there are many coconut palms and manchineel trees, which also provide shade. The numerous palm trees include the splendid royal palm.

Flowering shrubs provide beautiful colourful displays in gardens, parks and hotel grounds throughout the island. These include bougainvillea, Barbados pride, hibiscus, oleander,

A palm provides shade by the road along the beach

heliconia, poinsettias and petreas. Many flowers, such as roses, orchids, lilies and begonias, bloom throughout the year. In moist and shady areas there are many fruit trees, including the golden apple, mango, sour sop, guava, cherry, star apple and akee. The large breadfruit tree is common. It is reputed to have been introduced to the West Indies by Captain Bligh in 1793.

There is not a great variety of animals in Barbados. The green monkey, originally introduced from West Africa is still found, especially in the east of the island, although its survival is threatened. Other wild animals include the hare and the mongoose. The latter was introduced during the late nineteenth century to get rid of rats which damaged the sugar crop. Unlike other Caribbean islands, Barbados has only two types of snake,

Colourful displays are provided by Barbados' many flowers and shrubs, including orchids and oleanders

both of which are harmless. Other creatures include lizards, giant toads and the whistling frog which is tiny but makes a surprisingly loud and shrill noise during the night.

A number of species of bird live in Barbados. The most common include the yellow breast, grass finch, golden warbler, wood dove, sparrow, blackbird, parakeet and the tiny humming-bird. A number of birds, such as the frigate bird, brown pelican and sandpiper, visit the island in winter.

Insect life is abundant in Barbados, with cockroaches and houseflies being the greatest nuisance in the home. Ants, termites and crickets are common, as are centipedes and mosquitoes. Other pests include millipedes and scorpions.

Fish abound in the waters which surround the island, Perhaps the best known is the flying fish, given its name because of its habit of leaping and gliding above the surface of the waves. The shallow waters around the coral reefs teem with thousands of tiny colourful tropical fish.

Barbadians are becoming increasingly aware of the need to conserve the natural beauty of their island. There are several areas where plants and animals are preserved. Welchman Hall Gully in St Thomas, for example, is a ravine filled with tropical trees, plants and ferns. It is protected by the Barbados National Trust. Other areas include the Flower Forest in St Joseph, the privately-owned Andromeda Gardens near Bathsheba, and the

A view of the Scotland District which is designated a national park and includes Barbados' last remaining natural forest

Animal Flower Cave in St Lucy. In addition, the entire Scotland District forms a national park. This includes Turner's Hall Wood, the last area of original forest left in Barbados.

However, there are areas of Barbados where the plants and animals remain at risk. One such area is the Graeme Hall swamp in Christ Church—the only place where mangroves are found on the island. It has been suggested that this and other special areas should be made into nature reserves. Perhaps most pressingly, the delicate coral reefs which surround the island also require careful protection if they are not to be damaged by pollution.

Industry

Up to the middle of the 1950s, there had been little or no industry in Barbados. Some women did work at home producing goods on a cottage industry basis, for example, sewing and making clothes. In fact, Barbados still has a strong reputation for these products. But, in the past, there was very little other industry.

In order to encourage the development of factories, in 1957, the Barbados Development Board was set up. This independent body still exists and carries out the same task today. But, in 1969, it was given the new name of the Industrial Development Corporation or IDC. During the same period, a series of laws was passed which aimed to attract industries from other countries. The laws meant that such industries did not have to pay full taxes for some time after arriving in the country. Further, they did not have to pay import duty on goods and materials they imported into the country to carry out their manufacturing work.

Factories on an industrial estate developed by the Industrial Development Corporation of Barbados

It was hoped that this would encourage firms from more developed countries, such as America and Canada, to set up factories in Barbados. It was also anticipated that the stable government of the country along with the existence of a well-educated, trained and relatively inexpensive labour force would attract firms. The IDC named the entire campaign "Operation Beehive", because it involved "Busy Bs", or Barbadian workers.

The government set about building factories in special areas called industrial estates, and from 1959 to 1980, the Industrial Development Corporation built nine estates in various parts of the island. The first three were all in and around Bridgetown. They are known as the Grazettes, Harbour and Pelican estates. The Pelican estate is located between the deepwater harbour

70

and the city centre, and it sells locally-made craft items to visitors and residents. Somewhat later, in 1970, another estate was built in the Pine area of Bridgetown.

But, since 1964, the remaining new industrial estates have all been built outside the Bridgetown city area. The first was established in the northern parish of St Lucy, with a single large factory which makes clothes. Three estates were then built in the Christ Church area: the Newtown, Wildey and Grantley Adams industrial estates. One other estate of this type was built in the south-east of the country at Six Cross Roads in the parish of St Philip. These developments have all been part of the government's efforts to move facilities, jobs and people away from Bridgetown.

A sign showing the site of another IDC project

But despite this, nearly all the industrial estates are found in the already built-up areas of St Michael and Christ Church. Only the estates of St Lucy and Six Cross Roads in St Philip are located outside this area. In 1981, the building of a tenth industrial park was announced. It was to be developed just to the north of Speightstown at Six Men's. But, as yet, this has not been constructed.

The policy of developing industries has proved to be a success in a number of ways. In 1985, there were around three hundred industrial plants operating in Barbados. These were mainly of the type described as light industry, and they fell into two major groups. First, there are factories making foods for local use, like soft drinks, beer, biscuits and sweets. Secondly, there are more general manufacturing plants making furniture, mattresses, textiles, garments, plastics, medical equipment and pharmaceuticals. This group also includes the assembly of transistor radios and computer parts, as well as tourist handicrafts of various kinds.

Industry now provides jobs for over fifteen thousand people, that is almost fifteen per cent of the total workforce of the nation. The export of clothes and electrical parts earns Barbados a great deal of money, much more than it now receives from the sale of its sugar overseas. As a result of these changes, Barbados is now classified as an "industrializing" country. In fact, industry makes up about twelve per cent of the total production of Barbados.

But there are some critics who stress what they see as the less desirable things about industry. Firstly, many of the industries attracted from abroad provide relatively few jobs. It is argued that firms only come to Barbados in order to take advantage of the cheap wages and tax-free period. When economic problems occur, these overseas plants or "branch plants" are usually the first to be closed, leaving people without jobs once again.

There are few other industries in Barbados. About seven per cent of the workforce is engaged in building and construction work. The only heavy industrial plant was opened in 1986. This is the Arawak factory which makes cement. It was built as a joint Barbados-Trinidad project. Apart from this, there is still a small pottery industry based on the local clays in the Chalky Mount area. Similarly, bricks and tiles have been made in the Scotland district.

Barbados produces its own oil. Prospecting for petroleum started in 1919, but production has never exceeded fifteen hundred barrels a day. The wells from which it is produced are located to the south-east of the centre of the island, at the Woodbourne Oilfield. The oil produced is enough to supply about one-third of the island's total needs. A small oil refinery is located in northern Bridgetown. Here imported crude oil is used together with that from Barbados to produce gasolene, kerosene, diesel oil and fuel oil. The products are mainly used locally.

In the future, to continue the growth of its industrial sector, Barbados will probably have to attract industries which are based

**A view of the
Woodbourne Oilfield
which produces about
one-third of Barbados'
total oil needs**

on middle- to high-technology. Typical of these activities are the fast-growing industries of computer software and data analysis. Whether such efforts are likely to be as successful as those of the last twenty years remains to be seen. But there is no doubting the fact that today, light manufacturing and tourism have become the most important sectors of the Barbadian economy.

74

Tourism

Barbados has attracted tourists to its shores for a long time. One of the most famous people to visit the island was the American President George Washington. He came in 1751, and it was the only place he ever visited outside the United States.

But it was not until the twentieth century that any but the very rich could afford to travel to the Caribbean islands for holidays. It was the growth of modern sea and air travel which made it possible for more people to visit islands such as Barbados. Even in 1955, only fifteen thousand people visited the country. But the growth of tourism was very rapid during the 1960s and 1970s. In 1974, 230,000 visitors were recorded and, by 1980, this had risen to 370,000. The 400,000 level was passed for the first time in 1986.

Along with manufacturing industry, tourism now contributes more to the Barbados economy than sugar. Visitors come from Canada and the United States, as well as from Britain and Europe, where the winters are relatively cold. However, there

Scuba-diving off the west coast of Barbados

are now increasing numbers visiting from South America and from the other Caribbean islands.

The many attractions of Barbados include the warm climate, almost constant sunshine, blue skies and pleasant cooling breezes. Along with the white coral beaches fringed by swaying palms, they provide the typical image of a tropical island paradise.

The calm sheltered west coast with its blue waters and coral reefs offers visitors the opportunity to relax in the sunshine. Those who are more energetic can swim, snorkel, scuba-dive, sail and enjoy all kinds of water sports. In addition, the inland scenery of rolling hills, the historic sites and the wild Atlantic coast are also attractions for the visitor.

The growth of tourism to Barbados was greatly helped by the building of the deepwater harbour. Now, cruise-ships call regularly on their journeys through the Caribbean, bringing yet more short-stay visitors to the island—as many as 145,335 in 1986. The development of Grantley Adams International Airport has also encouraged tourism, bringing people to the island in large "jumbo" jets.

The Barbadian government has also promoted tourism. It set up the Tourist Development Board and this offered tax relief to businessmen building hotels and apartments. They were also allowed to import building materials and furnishings. Today, there are 13,500 bed-spaces available for tourists. And the tourist facilities, including many beaches, have been greatly improved.

Cruise-ships in the deepwater harbour at Bridgetown

A west-coast hotel

Many hotels, among them the most expensive ones, have been built along the west coast of the island. As a result, this area is called the Gold or Platinum Coast. Less expensive hotels and most self- catering apartments are found along the southern coast. Although the rugged east coast is very attractive to visitors, the government has discouraged the building of hotels along it.

Obviously, the arrival of large numbers of visitors in a small island has many effects. Some aspects of tourism, mainly the economic ones, have brought benefits to Barbados. But there are others which some people think have resulted in problems for the country.

On the positive side, Barbados has earned a great deal of money from tourism. This has helped greatly the government's

78

efforts to balance the economy. Some fifteen thousand jobs have been created directly, thereby helping to reduce unemployment. Work for taxi-drivers, local crafts-people and others has also been provided.

But there are difficulties that may stem from tourism, including economic ones. If there are world economic problems, such as a recession, then people tend to cut back on holidays and places like Barbados are badly hit as a result. In fact, this very thing happened during the 1970s.

Another point that needs to be considered is that the money made from tourism may not always spread to the local people. This is because many hotels are owned by large foreign companies. Also, a great deal of money is spent on importing the types of foods that tourists are used to eating at home.

The large number of visitors places heavy demands on land, beach and sea resources in what is already a crowded island. On the west coast, for instance, so many hotels have been built between the highway and the coast that it is almost impossible to get even a glimpse of the Caribbean Sea. In 1981, the government restricted the further development of tourism along the south and west coasts.

Another problem is that the jobs provided by tourism are seasonal. Most tourists visit the island between November and April and fewer people are required to work in hotels and elsewhere at other times of the year. Also, the growth of the number of self-catering apartments in the 1970s has meant that fewer local people are provided with jobs.

The arrival of large numbers of tourists can also cause social problems for the local population. The display of wealth may upset people whose standard of living is much lower. There have even been fears that tourism will lead to an increase in crime. It may also be difficult for local communities to cope with different social habits, customs and ways of dressing. Such social problems have resulted in the claim that too much attention is being given to the needs of the tourist and too little to those of the local people. Barbadians have rightly pointed out that they should not be prevented from visiting the beaches and other areas that tourists use.

The Barbados Tourist Board is aware of these problems. In 1981, it ran a campaign calling for people to "Make a Friend for Barbados Today". More recently, street banners proclaimed "Tourism is Our Business. Let's Play Our Part". It is hoped that these reminders will encourage Barbadians to take a positive view of tourism.

It is certain however that tourism will remain a vital part of the Barbadian economy. It appears that the task ahead for the government is to find the right balance between the level of tourism and its effects on the island community.

Culture, Religion, Sport and Pastimes

The culture of Barbados today is a combination of English and African ways. It is fair to say that, before independence, English ideas and ways of life were regarded as the most important. But slowly, over the last few years, fresh pride and interest have been shown in African ways of doing things. This is often referred to as the "African cultural heritage", and it is likely to continue to be very important in the future. Since 1960, however, North American ways have become ever more influential.

One of the things that Barbadians are very proud about is their standard of education. This is still largely based on the English system of schooling. Official figures show that ninety-eight per cent of the population can read and write. However, some argue that this very high figure is somewhat exaggerated.

On the other hand, nobody can doubt that Barbadians take education very seriously as a way of getting on in the world. On school days, pupils in neat and colourful uniforms can be seen making their way to one of the over one hundred government

Schoolgirls. Barbadians are proud of their standard of education

primary schools or twenty-one secondary schools. Education has been free in all government-run schools since 1962. In addition, around twenty per cent of pupils attend independent or privately-run schools.

One of the three campuses of the University of the West Indies has been built in Barbados. This is situated at Cave Hill on the northern edge of Bridgetown. It opened at its present site in 1967. Today, it has faculties of Arts, Natural Sciences, Law, Medicine and Social Sciences, an Institute of Social and

82

Economic Research and a School of Education. Currently, just over fifteen hundred students attend the Cave Hill campus, some of them coming from other Caribbean islands.

There are a number of other colleges. One is the Barbados Community College which opened in 1969, and provides education at the pre-university level. Another is the Samuel Jackson Prescod Polytechnic which was founded at around the same time.

The English settlers also brought their religion with them. Thus, today, Anglicanism or the Church of England is the established religion, with well in excess of half the population following it. But a very large number of other religions are present on the island, even though some of them have only small followings. The larger groups include the Methodists, Pentecostalists, Roman Catholics, Seventh Day Adventists, Moravians, Hindus, Muslims and followers of the Church of God.

There are over seventy churches on the island. Many of them, such as that in the parish of St John, date back to the early settlement of the island, and are of fine architectural style. For many people, religion plays a very important part in their lives. Sunday is still seen as a very special day; all over the island, people can be seen making their way to church to worship.

Some aspects of religion can also be traced back to African origins. One is called Obeah. It is a form of witchcraft or magic which involves spells and charms which are used by the Obeah man either for good or ill. Another more modern development

83

which relates to the African origins of the majority of the population is Rastafarianism. This was introduced to Barbados in the 1970s from Jamaica and has become quite popular with some young people. Rastafarians do not cut their hair; they wear it as long "dreadlocks". They regard the late Emperor Haile Selassie of Ethiopia as their spiritual leader. The red, green and gold of the Ethiopian flag are the badge of the movement and its "back to Africa" theme. Reggae music, as played by people like the Jamaican Bob Marley, has become deeply associated with the Rasta movement.

Festivals and "fetes" are another very important part of the cultural life of Barbados. These include the Holetown Festival held in February which celebrates the first settlement of the island, and the Oistins Fish Festival in April each year. In addition, many villages hold their own street fair or fete once every year.

By far the most important event is the Crop Over Festival held in July every year. Its origins lie in the days when slaves held a big party on the plantations at the end of the sugar-harvest. This celebration was revived as a national event in 1974. During the festival, the "King and Queen of the Crop" are chosen—they are the man and woman who have cut the largest number of canes. The climax of the whole celebration is called Kadooment Day—a national holiday, during which costumed bands parade in the streets after first gathering at the National Stadium on the outskirts of Bridgetown.

Celebrating the Crop Over Festival in July

The highlight of the Crop Over Festival is the crowning of the Calypso King each year. Calypso music has its origins in the slave songs brought from West Africa, although the modern form of this music was developed in Trinidad. Calypsos are catchy songs which have a strong rhythm and beat. Often the words are about current social happenings and the actions of politicians. Each year the leading Barbadian calypsonians, with names such as the Mighty Gabby and Red Plastic Bag, compete for this prized title.

Music is important at other social meetings. Tuk bands, made up of groups of strolling minstrels, play music with a fast beat as they move from place to place. Often the band is joined by a man

A tuk band on the beach (the drum sounds *boom-a-tuk, boom-a-tuk*)

dressed as a donkey, and sometimes by men dressed in women's clothing. Tuk bands typically play at festivals, picnics, excursions and public holidays.

Another interesting feature of Afro-Barbadian culture is the "Landship" Movement which was originated by a Barbadian seaman in the 1870s. This is a club which is organized and structured like a ship—but with a vital difference—it exists on the land. The members of the "crew" wear various navy-style uniforms when they parade and dance. The dances are performed to tuk band music.

The Barbados Arts Council was created in 1957 and its task is to encourage different forms of art. There are now a number of active painters on the island who depict its scenery and people. Karl Broodhagen is a well-known Barbadian sculptor. His statue of the *Freed Slave* commemorating the one hundred and fiftieth anniverary of emancipation is seen by many as a masterpiece. There are a number of art galleries where paintings are regularly put on show. One of these is the National Cultural Foundation Gallery at Queen's Park in Bridgetown.

In the past few years, creative dance has once again become important in Barbados. Dance was an essential part of the culture of West African slaves. This tradition is being actively developed by modern dance troupes such as the Barbados Dance Theatre Company. There are also frequent amateur drama productions. One well-established theatre group is called the Green Room Players.

Recently, drama, dance and song have come together in the

A mural depicting the country's pastimes, sports and culture

form of dinner shows for tourists. These tell the story of the history of the island. One is called *1627 and all that* and is performed at the Barbados Museum. Another *Barbados Barbados* is enacted at Balls Plantation.

With regard to writing and literature too, Barbados is making significant contribution to West Indian culture. One of the best-known works by a Barbadian is George Lamming's novel *In the Castle of My Skin*, which is based on his childhood experiences of growing up on the island. There are also many other writers producing novels, poetry and short stories.

Barbadian people do many things with their spare time. Often they give what are called "Grand Dances". This means that they hold a dance party and invite other people to attend on a paying basis. These dances are generally held at weekends. Forth-coming dance parties are advertised in the newspapers. Normally a photograph of the organizer appears with an invitation starting "Hi there, friends and dance fans!"

But, as in many other countries, playing and watching sport is perhaps the major pastime in Barbados. And one sport, cricket, can only be described as the national sport and obsession. Indeed, some years ago, the politician Sir Grantley Adams said that "cricket is the religion of Barbados". Certainly, few who have visited the island would dispute this claim. The home of cricket is the Kensington Oval located to the north-west of the city centre of Bridgetown. It dates from 1822. Here, test matches and other international games are played.

A cricket match in progress on the Cave Hill campus of the University of the West Indies in northern Bridgetown

Cricket is, of course, a legacy of the English period. But what is remarkable is that over the years such a small island, no more than the size of a single English city, has managed to produce so many world-class cricketers. In the 1950s, there were the "Three Terrible W's"—Frank Worrell, Clyde Walcott and Everton Weekes. Frank Worrell was knighted and is now pictured on the island's $5 note.

Undoubtedly, the best-known Barbadian cricketer and undisputed king is the former all-rounder Garfield Sobers. Gary Sobers was knighted by the Queen of England in 1975. Barbados has also produced more than its fair share of fast bowlers, and names such as Charlie Griffith, Wesley Hall and more recently, Joel (Big Bird) Garner and Malcolm Marshall have struck fear

89

into the hearts of batsmen of many nations all over the world.

Another increasingly popular sport is soccer. Teams with English-sounding names like Spurs, United and Everton compete each week in an organized league. Other well-established sports include horse-racing at the Garrison Savannah, basketball, volleyball, tennis, table tennis, weight-lifting, body-building and motor rallying. And the game of dominoes is played by men here, there and everywhere, especially in and around rum shops during the evenings.

With over twenty years having passed since independence, there is every sign that Barbados, although a small country, has a culture and tradition of its own. There is a new and healthy respect for things which stem from the African origins of the majority of the population. Increasingly, it is possible to talk of an active and growing Afro-Barbadian culture.

The Future: "Little America"?

Barbados has come a long way. It is now regarded as a more developed country within the Third World. Tourism, manufacturing industry and other activities have contributed to economic progress and national self-assurance. Barbados has also made contributions in fields such as culture and sport.

The political ties with England, the former colonial power, have been cut. On 30 November, 1987, Barbados "came of age", reaching twenty-one years of independent self-government. An Independence Arch was built in central Bridgetown to mark the occasion. Undoubtedly, traces of the former English presence are still there for all to see, and Barbados remains an active member of the Commonwealth. But to regard Barbados as "Little England" in the latter part of the twentieth century would be wrong. For one thing, the recent pride in African "roots" is leading to new ways of thinking and doing things.

But it has to be faced that, like all Caribbean countries, on the world scale, Barbados is very small. It is therefore dependent to a greater or lesser extent on larger and more powerful countries, in particular the United States of America and Canada.

At various times in the past, Caribbean countries have considered joining together into larger groups in order to make them more powerful. This was true of the efforts to form a West Indian Confederation as early as 1876. In 1958, Barbados became a part of the West Indies Federation, but this failed in 1962. Barbados is now a member of CARIFTA, the Caribbean Free Trade Asssociation, and CARICOM, the Caribbean Community and Common Market. These were established in 1973 and 1968 respectively and are aimed at bringing Caribbean countries closer together.

But, in all aspects of life, the last twenty years have seen the growth of very strong links between Barbados and North America. For example, the largest number of holiday-makers come from Canada and the United States. These two countries have provided loans and aid for many development projects. Increasingly, well-off Barbadians travel to North America for vacations. More importantly, many now go there in order to study and to work. Increasingly, these two-way links are affecting the everyday life and culture of Barbados. It affects things like the food Barbadians eat, the clothes they wear, the way they do their shopping and the television programmes they watch.

As a result, some people might argue that Barbados is fast becoming "Little America". Certainly, despite its landscape, history and everyday life, this seems a more appropriate

92

Barbadian children. They are growing up in an independent nation which reflects influences from Africa, England, the United States and the remainder of the Caribbean

description of Barbados today, than the "Little England" of the past.

Now, however, Barbados seems to be well set to create its own identity for the future. As well as reflecting distinct Caribbean and North American influences, this is certain to include some aspects of its strong African and English traditions.

Index

94